STEPPENWOLF

Hermann Hesse

TECHNICAL DIRECTOR Maxwell Krohn
EDITORIAL DIRECTOR Justin Kestler
MANAGING EDITOR Ben Florman

SERIES EDITORS Boomie Aglietti, Justin Kestler
PRODUCTION Christian Lorentzen, Camille Murphy

WRITERS Mei Pin Phua, Monica Ferrell
EDITORS Benjamin Morgan, Matt Blanchard

This edition published by Spark Publishing

Spark Publishing
A Division of SparkNotes LLC
120 Fifth Avenue, 8th Floor
New York, NY 10011

02 03 04 05 SN 9 8 7 6 5 4 3 2 1

Please send all comments and questions or report errors to
feedback@sparknotes.com.

Library of Congress information available upon request

Printed and bound in the United States

RRD-C

ISBN 1-58663-491-7

INTRODUCTION: STOPPING TO BUY SPARKNOTES ON A SNOWY EVENING

Whose words these are you *think* you know.
Your paper's due tomorrow, though;
We're glad to see you stopping here
To get some help before you go.

Lost your course? You'll find it here.
Face tests and essays without fear.
Between the words, good grades at stake:
Get great results throughout the year.

Once school bells caused your heart to quake
As teachers circled each mistake.
Use SparkNotes and no longer weep,
Ace every single test you take.

Yes, books are lovely, dark, and deep,
But only what you grasp you keep,
With hours to go before you sleep,
With hours to go before you sleep.

Contents

CONTEXT   I

PLOT OVERVIEW   3

CHARACTER LIST   5

ANALYSIS OF MAJOR CHARACTERS   7
   THE STEPPENWOLF (HARRY HALLER)   7
   HERMINE   7
   PABLO   8

THEMES, MOTIFS & SYMBOLS   9
   MULTIPLE IDENTITIES   9
   THE EXISTENCE OF A WORLD BEYOND TIME   9
   THE COMPLEX NATURE OF LAUGHTER   10
   MUSIC   11
   DANCING   11
   REPRESENTATION   11
   MIRRORS   12
   THE RADIO   13
   THE ARAUCARIA PLANT   13

SUMMARY & ANALYSIS   15
   PREFACE   15
   THE FIRST PART OF HARRY HALLER'S RECORDS   18
   THE SECOND PART OF HARRY HALLER'S RECORDS   22
   THE THIRD PART OF HARRY HALLER'S RECORDS   26
   THE FOURTH PART OF HARRY HALLER'S RECORDS   29
   THE FIFTH PART OF HARRY HALLER'S RECORDS   32
   THE SIXTH PART OF HARRY HALLER'S RECORDS   35

IMPORTANT QUOTATIONS EXPLAINED 41

KEY FACTS 46

STUDY QUESTIONS & ESSAY TOPICS 48

REVIEW & RESOURCES 52
    QUIZ 52
    SUGGESTIONS FOR FURTHER READING 57

NOTE: This SparkNote refers to the Henry Holt and Company / Owl Books edition of *Steppenwolf*, translated by Joseph Mileck and Horst Frenz.

CONTEXT

Hermann Hesse was born in 1877 in the Black Forest region of Germany. Hesse's family subscribed to Pietism, a Protestant religion that emphasizes heartfelt devotion and charitable activity rather than dogma. Various members of the family had been missionaries in India or religious publishers, and Hesse was expected to continue this religious legacy. He was sent to a monastery but left after a year.

As a youth, Hesse read voraciously and decided to become a writer. After years of struggling to publish his work, he gained acclaim with the novel *Peter Camenzind* (1904). Hesse became a staunch pacifist; during World War I, he moved to Montagnola, Switzerland, and eventually became a Swiss citizen.

Hesse found fame with the novels *Siddhartha* (1922), *Steppenwolf* (1927), and *Narcissus and Goldmund* (1930), all of which address the split between the world of physical sensation and the world of mental reasoning. Hesse's primary influences in these novels were German Romanticism, late-nineteenth-century aestheticism, and Indian and Chinese religious philosophy. In his novels, Hesse strove to reconcile the physical and spiritual elements of his characters, whose desires frequently involve transcending the realm of the individual and entering the realm of the universal spirit. The lives of Hesse's characters are generally uncomfortable, but his prose lends romance to their suffering.

The publication of *Steppenwolf* in 1927 caused a scandal, as the novel's candid accounts of the corrupt elements of a city disappointed readers who had become accustomed to Hesse's highly spiritual works. Critics claimed that the novel was too obviously confessional, as it sprang out of a crisis in Hesse's own life. He wrote the novel after the failure of his first marriage and the collapse of his brief second marriage. Indeed, Hesse, who was shy and had always felt most comfortable at home, had gone on something of a socializing rampage, frequenting the bars and dance halls of Zurich. He spent most of his days drinking alcohol and most of his nights writing self-pitying poems (written before, but published after, the publication of *Steppenwolf*). These poems, which offer a painfully honest record of Hesse's alcoholism, suicidal tendencies, and sense of mental and physical estrangement, serve as interesting companion pieces to the novel.

By the end of 1926, Hesse abandoned his self-indulgent lifestyle and retired to the solitude of his country retreat in Switzerland. Hesse's work fluctuated widely in popularity during his career and has continued to do so since. His outspokenly pacifist novels were vilified and banned in Nazi Germany but were celebrated after World War II. In America, the Beat generation of the 1950s and the hippies of the 1960s enthusiastically embraced Hesse's blend of Eastern philosophy and existentialism. Today, Hesse is acknowledged as one of the most influential German authors of the twentieth century, and he is widely respected for fusing elements of philosophies from around the globe in his work. Hesse's efforts earned him the Nobel Prize for Literature in 1946. He died in 1962 at his home in Switzerland.

Plot Overview

H ARRY HALLER, A MIDDLE-AGED INTELLECTUAL, moves into a lodging house in a medium-sized, generic town, which is never named. Despairing and melancholy, Harry feels himself to be "a wolf of the Steppes," or "Steppenwolf," adrift and alone in a world that is incomprehensible to him and offers him no joy. *Steppenwolf* recounts Harry's pain and anxiety as he tries to overcome his crippling sense of dislocation and despair at the futility of humanity.

Harry is repulsed by the productive, organized, and diligent optimism of the bourgeoisie, or middle class. Even so, he is bewitched by its charms. Caught between the urges of his wolf-half and his man-half, Harry can neither completely disavow nor embrace a conventional way of life. He regularly contemplates committing suicide.

One night, while Harry walks unhappily through an old quarter of the city, he sees a sign over a door he has never noticed before. The sign reads "MAGIC THEATER—ENTRANCE NOT FOR EVERYBODY." More letters reflected on the street spell out "FOR MADMEN ONLY!" Harry cannot open the door, but a sign-bearer advertising the Magic Theater gives Harry a booklet entitled "Treatise on the Steppenwolf." This booklet contains a precise description of the way Harry feels as a Steppenwolf. It speaks of a person who is half man and half wolf who hates the bourgeois lifestyle but who is also at the same time incapable of surrendering himself to the pleasure of the senses.

Harry soon becomes even more certain that he must kill himself immediately. At a professor's house, Harry gravely insults his former colleague about the way Goethe, the famous German poet, is represented in a portrait that hangs in his home. Feeling that he has at last severed all ties to humanity, Harry plans to commit suicide that evening. However, Harry meets an enchanting young girl in a tavern that night, and she gives him sensible and maternal advice. The two meet again the following week. Because the girl resembles a boyhood friend of Harry's named Herman, Harry guesses that she is called Hermine. He is correct. Hermine begins to help Harry. Grateful that she has broken through his isolation, he agrees to obey all her commands. Hermine informs Harry that eventually she will make him fall in love with her, then she will ask him to kill her.

Hermine teaches Harry to dance, finds him a lover named Maria, and introduces him to an enigmatic and beautiful jazz musician named Pablo. Through Hermine and her friends, Harry begins to immerse himself in a hedonistic, or pleasure-filled, way of life. He comes to appreciate all the sensual aspects of life he had previously disregarded because of his strict bourgeois upbringing. With Hermine and Maria, everything from buying little love gifts to picking duck meat from its bones becomes a delightful affair. Harry blooms and becomes happy during these weeks of change. Despite the enjoyment he feels, however, part of him remains repulsed by his transformation. Part of Harry continues to aspire toward the spiritual and the divine, away from the sordid pleasures of the flesh. When Harry confesses his feelings, he finds that Hermine understands him perfectly. In fact, she understands him better than he understands himself.

Harry's concerns peak at the Fancy Dress Ball, a gala masquerade dance Harry attends. After several hours of liberating, riotous revelry, Harry consummates his love with Hermine through a nuptial dance. As the ball comes to a close, Pablo invites Harry and Hermine to enjoy his Magic Theater. Pablo explains to Harry that the goal of the theater is the dissolution of the personality, a goal that can be accomplished only through laughter.

Once inside this "school of humor," Harry laughs at a mirror image of himself and goes down a corridor lined with dozens of strange doors, some of which he enters. Each door opens on a new, surreal world. Harry runs from one world, in which men and machines are engrossed in a bloody war, to another, where all the women he has ever wanted are available for him to enjoy.

Reality quickly falls away as the novel brings us deeper and deeper into the psyche of the Steppenwolf. Harry ends up in a room where he finds Hermine and Pablo's love-spent, naked bodies lying on the floor. Believing that the moment has come to fulfill his promise to kill Hermine, Harry stabs her with a knife that has magically appeared in his pocket. The celebrated classical composer Mozart appears and tells Harry that he has abused the Magic Theater with such excessively serious behavior. Mozart explains that life is always compromised and full of less-than-ideal circumstances, and that the task Harry must face now is to greet these aspects with laughter. Although Harry has failed this time, according to Pablo, he leaves the theater with the deep belief that one day he will get things right.

CHARACTER LIST

The Steppenwolf A middle-aged recluse who lives alone in a bourgeois lodging house. Harry Haller refers to himself as a "Steppenwolf" because he feels like a lonely wolf of the steppes, removed from the obsessions and conventions common to most people. Harry believes himself to be divided between two extremes: a man-half who shares the ideals and interests of humanity, and a beast-half that sees those aspirations as futile, absurd vanities.

Hermine A lovely young hedonist and courtesan. Hermine resembles Romantic stereotypes such as the Madonna-Sophia figure, the noble whore, and the loving sister. Since she looks extraordinarily like Harry's childhood friend Herman, we are led to believe that she is perhaps only a reflection of some part of Harry.

Maria Harry's blonde and blue-eyed lover. Maria is a creature of the senses, talented in all the intricate arts of love and as voracious as she is generous. Her love reenergizes Harry with new hope and vitality. Harry's love affair with Maria makes him fond of aspects of sexuality and romance that he previously had seen as degrading and trivial.

Pablo A jazz saxophone player and bandleader wildly popular among the denizens of the world of pleasure. Laconic and unabashedly modern, at first Pablo inspires the Steppenwolf only with disdain. Harry calls him a child with no worries. Pablo is the polar opposite of Harry, substituting with pleasure what Harry has in intellect.

Mozart The renowned classical composer. Harry, who has a lifelong obsession with Mozart, encounters him in the Magic Theater as the ultimate representative of "the immortals." This eccentric, personal Mozart is as modern as he is a man of the past, and is also thoroughly unceremonious and jocular.

The Editor The nephew of the Steppenwolf's landlady. The novel opens with a fictional preface by the Editor, to whom Harry has left his records, indicating he may do with them as he pleases. The Editor, a straightforwardly bourgeois individual, has respect and sympathy for Harry.

Analysis of Major Characters

The Steppenwolf (Harry Haller)

Hesse published *Steppenwolf* in 1927, after a failed marriage and two subsequent years of debauchery. Harry Haller's age, profession, intellectual interests, and unpopular pacifist journalism match Hesse's own. Hesse suggests that Harry is actually a reflection of himself. Just as the concept of "the Steppenwolf" is useful to Harry for self-analytical purposes, Harry is useful to Hesse as an illuminating fictional construction.

Harry is more like a theoretical framework than a believable, realistic character. He appears out of nowhere, inhabits a nameless space, and disappears again into nowhere when his usefulness evaporates. Harry is also an engaging character. The more mundane aspects of his existence—his admiration of his favorite wine, his embarrassment about his aging, his physical sufferings—are refreshingly lifelike and endearing. These touches soften Harry's seemingly boundless despair and self-absorption.

Hermine

The lovely and generous Hermine takes Harry under her wing and teaches him to live, putting him in touch with his long-ignored sensuous side. As a hedonistic young courtesan, Hermine is Harry's opposite in many ways, yet also his close double. She enters his life by a magical accident, as Harry goes to the Black Eagle tavern, where the signboard man of the Magic Theater directs him to go. As a result, from the start Hermine is clearly something more than a realistic character. Hesse reveals Hermine's magical, surreal aspects when Harry finds that she resembles his boyhood friend Herman and impossibly guesses that her name is a feminine version of his friend's.

The closing passages of the novel reveal that Hermine is actually a part of Harry. When Harry stabs her, her slain body neatly shrinks to the size of a figurine. Although it is never clear whether Harry

murders Hermine or merely a hallucination of her, the novel's closing words suggest that Hermine has always been only a reflection of
Harry. Once Harry has integrated back into his personality the life
of the body that he has hitherto repressed, Hermine is no longer
needed and is therefore dispelled. She serves as Harry's magic mirror, calling out of him and making visible those parts to which he
had previously been blind. When Harry learns to see himself clearly,
he effectively destroys Hermine.

PABLO

Pablo plays perhaps the most instrumental role in the changes that
occur in *Steppenwolf*. Clues to his importance are present from his
first mention in the narrative. Hermine foreshadows Pablo's importance in her extreme admiration for him and her claim that he can
play all instruments and speak all the languages of the world. The
fact that Pablo is the character most associated with music provides
a persistent cue to his significance. Indeed, he is a genius bandleader
and therefore in charge of defining the rhythms to which all others
must tune their behavior. Yet, despite Harry's efforts to discover
Pablo's value, we have little to go on until the very close of the novel,
when Pablo introduces Harry to the Magic Theater.

In the Magic Theater, the seemingly simple-minded Pablo
achieves his apotheosis, revealing himself to be the most enlightened
figure in the story. In fact, an earlier criticism of Pablo—that he
seemed unproblematic as a child—turns out to be a marker of his
profound wisdom. Pablo's wisdom does not require the stifling
books and theories under which Harry has buried half his life.
Rather, Pablo's wisdom stems from lived experience, and from a
deep consideration of the world that exists within one's own soul.
As Pablo explains to Harry, the important thing is to play music and
play it well—not to waste time talking or theorizing about it. Pablo's
ability to shift effortlessly between his two saxophones as he plays
symbolizes the ideal integration of the spiritual and the physical to
which Harry aspires.

THEMES, MOTIFS & SYMBOLS

THEMES

Themes are the fundamental and often universal ideas explored in a literary work.

MULTIPLE IDENTITIES

Steppenwolf describes Harry Haller's unusual, tragic condition. He is torn between two selves: a man-half who desires the respectability and comforts of bourgeois existence, and a wolf-half who scoffs at these vain, absurd desires. Although Hesse returns to this dichotomy throughout the novel, he also frequently dismisses it as overly simplistic and exaggerated. According to the "Treatise on the Steppenwolf," the idea that Harry is composed of these two selves is useful in theory, but, like all such theoretical constructs, is ultimately unable to capture the complexity and richness of reality. According to the Treatise, "Harry consists of a hundred or a thousand selves, not of two." Moreover, this is true not only in Harry's case but is an inherent condition of mankind.

The idea of multiple identities is most fully explored in the Magic Theater at the novel's close. Pablo speaks of the theater as a place in which to perform the dissolution of the personality. Behind one of the strange doors, a man closely resembling Pablo teaches Harry that the individual is comprised of innumerable selves that may be reconfigured in varying ways, like chess pieces. Drawing upon the Eastern ideas of reincarnation and transmigration of the soul into infinite bodies, and upon the psychoanalytic theories of Carl Jung, Hesse articulates a highly personal hypothesis of the multifaceted nature of the soul.

THE EXISTENCE OF A WORLD BEYOND TIME

In her most intense and revealing discussion with Harry, on the day before the Fancy Dress Ball, Hermine emphasizes something she calls "eternity." Eternity exists "at the back of time." It is the realm of all the things that matter—works of genius by artists like Mozart,

9

the strength and potency within all true feelings and acts, and the pure saints and suffering martyrs.

Hermine's speech provides the clearest formulation of Hesse's idea of such a world beyond time. Other figures in *Steppenwolf* refer to it in more or less straightforward terms; Goethe for instance, speaks of the mistake man commits in making too much of time. Indeed, the mere fact of Harry's encounters with past geniuses points to their continuing existence in some realm freed from the mechanism of time. More subtly, the idea of existence beyond time crops up as a frequent sensation whenever Harry is operating correctly. Caught up in the collective dancing fervor at the ball, for instance, Harry says that he has "lost the sense of time."

Since *Steppenwolf* is meant to be an educational text, Hesse develops the idea of a world beyond in tandem with his other major ideas in the novel. The laughter of the "immortals" is one way of entering into the world of eternity. Likewise, the failure to recognize the existence of multiple selves within the individual may be linked to an insufficient consciousness of timelessness. Indeed, when Harry looks into the gigantic mirror of the Magic Theater, he sees dozens of Harrys of all sizes, inclinations, and temperaments. One Harry even darts off impetuously before Harry's astonished eyes. Being thus intertwined with the other major ideas of the novel, the existence of a space beyond time in a sense provides the soul of these ideas. Laughter may offer a way to confront life, but it is eternity that holds the key to the reason for doing so. Hesse suggests that our actions struggling on behalf of goodness and genius do matter in the large-scale view.

THE COMPLEX NATURE OF LAUGHTER

Steppenwolf recounts the drama of a conflicted, despairing individual's quest to resolve his internal difficulties so that he may once again live life. The novel offers a straightforward solution to this problem: laughter. Each source of wisdom in the story—the "Treatise on the Steppenwolf," Goethe, Hermine, Pablo, and Mozart—advises Harry that laughter is the correct approach to life. Laughter tinkles coldly and beautifully at all of the novel's most intense, breakthrough moments, and the story finally closes on Harry's determined resolution to learn how to laugh.

Hesse's notion of laughter is complex. It is neither an escape from life into pleasure and entertainment nor a recasting of the darker sides of existence with an artificial rosy light. Rather, the laughter that the enlightened possess pierces through the serious traumas of existence while at the same time superseding and transcending them. Though Harry has been correct in finding human existence full of horrors, the appropriate response to this knowledge is not to destroy one's life through obsession with the ultimate failure. Instead, one must struggle and at the same time laugh at the world's mess.

MOTIFS

Motifs are recurring structures, contrasts, or literary devices that can help to develop and inform the text's major themes.

MUSIC

Harry's profound attachment to music is obvious from the start, when the preface describes the curious changes that come over him at the symphony. Harry's earliest and greatest idol is Mozart. Among Harry's greatest frustrations with modern popular culture are the radio and gramophone, which he dislikes because he believes they defile sacred music. For Harry, music floats above the world of mundane realities, a perfect, transcendent sphere of the spiritual. This high estimation of music recalls German Romantic aesthetic theory, which prized music foremost among the arts because it does not attempt to represent something else, as visual or dramatic arts do. Strictly pure, divorced from having to picture or describe any physical thing, music seems to belong to the divine world beyond the visible one.

DANCING

The motif of dancing operates alongside the motif of music. If music provides a sense of the immortal, lofty spiritual world, dancing suggests a tuning of earthly actions to the rhythms of the divine. Hermine teaches Harry to dance and at the same time teaches him how to combine physical and spiritual life. The fact that Pablo is a genius bandleader, choosing and directing the songs to which a multitude dances, reflects his gift for bringing the two parts of the self—the sensuous and the spiritual—into harmony.

REPRESENTATION

Steppenwolf is full of many kinds of representations. The novel contains a multitude of different narrative representations of Harry, from the preface of his landlady's nephew, to Harry's own records, to the "Treatise on the Steppenwolf," to the poems Harry pens in the course of the novel. Each narrative representation of Harry possesses its own limited share of truth. None contains the whole truth of Harry, yet each elucidates some aspect of his character. Harry himself notes this when he looks at the Treatise and a bit of his own writing. Exploring representation in this way, Hesse emphasizes his assertion that an individual is not a simplistic unit but a rich complexity of thousands of souls.

Though some representations in the novel are truthful but incomplete, many are simply inadequate. The most striking of these is the portrait of Goethe, which incites Harry's self-righteous fervor. As Hermine points out, in his outburst Harry has committed the same error of which he accused the professor's wife. If no one knows what Goethe really looked like, Harry's own cherished image of the poet is just as subjective and self-serving as the portrait. Hermine's criticism demonstrates that all representations are interpretations, each from a different angle. Each representation, though sometimes successful in its own way, is also inevitably limited.

SYMBOLS

Symbols are objects, characters, figures, or colors used to represent abstract ideas or concepts.

MIRRORS

In a novel concerned with the discovery of the self and its pluralities, mirrors occupy a central symbolic niche. The voyage in the Magic Theater is one long look into a hallucinatory fun-house mirror. Even the "Treatise on the Steppenwolf" may be seen as a mirror made of words, one that speaks back to Harry specifically. Of the novel's other, subtler mirrors, Hermine is the most important. She recognizes her mirroring function, declaring that she serves as Harry's much-needed looking glass. Harry himself later notes that gazing at Hermine is like gazing into a mirror. Yet, as much as Hermine reflects Harry, she also draws out of him those aspects of himself to which he has previously been blind. Articulating the feelings that are hidden inside Harry, Hermine draws out both the expression of these feelings and Harry's realization of their existence.

THE RADIO

Harry's relationship to the radio—the quintessential incarnation of the shabby mediocrity of modern life—is fraught with distrust, disgust, and foreboding. Harry distrusts the radio's warping of music, and feels disgusted that the general populace tolerates and fails to notice such defilement. Harry's negative feelings blind him to any positive interpretation of the radio, as we see in his conversation with his landlady over tea. After touching on some of the interesting philosophical implications of the radio, Harry quickly gets sidetracked into an angry polemic.

THE ARAUCARIA PLANT

Harry sees the araucaria plant in the vestibule of an apartment in his lodging house as the ultimate symbol of bourgeois order and moderation. Everything about the plant, which is spotlessly clean and obviously cared for devotedly, bespeaks the routines and rhythms of bourgeois life. Harry experiences nostalgia for such a life, but he also feels excluded from it. The araucaria is thus both a beacon of a lost world and a symbol of the narrow-minded, shortsighted bourgeoisie that Harry scorns.

SYMBOLS

Summary & Analysis

Preface

SUMMARY
The narrator explains that the work to follow constitutes the records of a man who called himself the Steppenwolf, the "wolf of the Steppes." The narrator identifies himself as the nephew of the landlady of the lodging house where the Steppenwolf spent nine or ten months before mysteriously disappearing. The narrator assures us that the portrait of the Steppenwolf that the records provide is fuller and more detailed than the one that emerged from the narrator's slight encounters with the man. He says that the Steppenwolf was an extremely shy and antisocial being, a man so lonely and so strange that he seemed to come from another world altogether.

The narrator recounts his brief run-ins with the Steppenwolf. When the Steppenwolf first arrives at the narrator's aunt's lodging house, he sniffs the air and declares that it smells good. The narrator becomes suspicious and repulsed when the Steppenwolf asks that the police not be informed of his arrival. The narrator's disgust heightens over time as he observes the Steppenwolf's unusual books, odd hours, heavy drinking, and incessant smoking. These habits are all most disagreeable to the strictly bourgeois narrator. However, his aunt's spirited defense of the Steppenwolf, along with the narrator's own positive, interesting encounters with the man, leads him to view the Steppenwolf sympathetically, as a rare, sensitive individual. However, the narrator adds that the effect of his exposure to the Steppenwolf has been "disturbing and disquieting."

The narrator tells us that the Steppenwolf's real name is Harry Haller. He describes a look that the Steppenwolf gives him during a lecture given by a very famous speaker. This look, according to the narrator, pierces not only the speaker's own arrogance but also the self-deluding, pompous, and flawed nature of the entire epoch. The narrator believes that Haller is deeply intelligent and insightful, but that his gifts lead to his overwhelming loneliness and propensity to suffer. The narrator goes on to call the Steppenwolf a "genius of suffering" in the manner of Nietzsche, the renowned nineteenth-century German philosopher. He then speculates that perhaps Haller experienced a traumatically repressive upbringing, which has made him hate himself.

The narrator offers an account of the Steppenwolf's habits, describing one particular encounter that stands out. Returning home one day, the narrator finds Haller seated on the landing of the stairs between the first and second floors. Haller admits that he is fascinated by the sight and smell of the incredible middle-class cleanliness that is manifest in the perfectly maintained araucaria plant on the landing. The plant is situated next to a spotlessly clean vestibule at the entrance of a first-floor flat. Haller insists that he does not speak with irony and instead expresses nostalgia for his own long-lost bourgeois existence.

Haller invites the narrator to join him in his apartment, where he reads and comments on a quotation out of one of his books. The quotation describes how men will not "swim before they are able to." Haller takes the idea of swimming to refer to a life of profound thought, telling the narrator that most men prefer solid earth and are "made for life, not for thought." Those who do go far in thought barter away their hold on solid earth, and each will one day drown.

The narrator then describes a time when he saw Haller at the symphony and recalls that Haller reacted very curiously to the music. During the first and third pieces, the Steppenwolf seemed in a vacant, irritated frame of mind, taken up by other thoughts. During the second piece, however, Haller bloomed and seemed transported by the music into a state of clear rapture. The narrator also recounts seeing a pretty young woman twice visit Haller. Though Haller and the woman seem to go out together happily, both times Haller returns alone in a forlorn state. The third time the woman visits, she and Haller quarrel terribly.

The narrator claims that although Haller was obviously very depressed and in bad shape, he does not believe that Haller has killed himself. The narrator states that the manuscript that follows has been left to him, and that although he is powerless to verify its accuracy, he believes that it reflects the Steppenwolf's spiritual journey. He adds that these records, despite their at times disgusting content, are valuable because they are representative of the times. The narrator alleges that they express not just the psychological distress of one man, but the social ailments of a whole age—or rather, the distress of that specific breed of man who is caught between two ages.

ANALYSIS

The preface has four primary functions: it endows the text with compelling realism, provides justification and support for its story, introduces the character of Harry Haller, and announces the book's major themes and motifs. The preface creates a strong sense of realism, suggesting that we are reading an actual document left behind by a real person. The fact that the name Harry Haller resembles the name Herman Hesse implies that Haller's records are autobiographical for Hesse. As *Steppenwolf* is often fantastical and macabre, the fact that the preface is told by an upstanding, solid, average citizen provides a seemingly factual context.

In addition to aiding in suspending the reader's disbelief, the preface also makes a strong case that justifies and supports the novel. The narrator's claim that the manuscript is valuable functions as a less-than-subtle claim that Hesse's novel is likewise valuable. Moreover, in agreeing with Haller's self-conception of being a wolf from the steppes, the narrator affirms the painful confessions and self-criticisms we encounter in Haller's own words. The fair, steadfast, and practical-minded nephew slowly comes to empathize with Haller as "a genius of suffering." Because we can identify with the nephew, who gradually gains an appreciation of the Steppenwolf, we as readers make the same shift, coming to empathize with Haller and his story.

The preface also lays down a brief sketch of the man whose complex inner life forms the action of the novel. We learn of Harry Haller's extreme dislocation, sense of estrangement, extraordinary intelligence, and sensitivity. Perhaps more important, the preface sets out the terms of the conflict in which the Steppenwolf sees himself caught. On the one hand, Haller is a disruptive wolf of the steppes, staying up late drinking wine and reading his colossally impractical books—generally living in a haphazard fashion. On the other hand, however, Haller also feels bound by a deep affection for the orderly bourgeois world to which he feels he can never belong. The fact that the outcome of this conflict is inevitably suffering, and that there is some value to this suffering—the nephew valorizes the Steppenwolf's suffering when he calls him a "genius" of it—are important assessments that we are obviously meant to adopt.

Finally, the preface introduces some of the major themes and motifs of Haller's existence. First, it invokes great thinkers such as Nietzsche, as Haller repeatedly tries to understand his own life in terms of his relation to the gifted cultural geniuses of the past. Second, through the rapture Haller experiences at the symphony and during his visits with the young woman, we see the power music and women have in transforming him. Third, we get a first glimpse of the symbolic contrast between solidity and fluidity. The quotation that Haller enthusiastically reads the narrator sets out a contrast between standing on the solid earth and being immersed in water. Hesse will repeatedly employ these two images in providing an allegory for Haller's actions. While standing on solid earth reflects bourgeois existence, an unproblematic attachment to worldly life, the immersion in water reflects those few hyperintelligent risk-takers who are unsatisfied by simple answers and devote themselves to the most profound thought.

THE FIRST PART OF HARRY HALLER'S RECORDS

"For Madmen Only" through the "Treatise on the Steppenwolf"

SUMMARY

[H]e knew all the time . . . that he was in reality not a man, but a wolf of the Steppes.
(See QUOTATIONS, p. 41)

Harry Haller's autobiographical records begin with a typical day, which Harry says he passes reading books and experiencing physical pain. His days, Harry explains, are mediocre and indistinguishable from one another. He passes from mild scholarly endeavors to bodily discomforts to the minor delights of a walk or warm bath. Harry is so unhappy with all of these experiences that he considers the option of escaping by committing suicide.

Harry rages against contentment, healthiness, and comfort, all of which he perceives to be part of the optimism of the middle class. However, he admits that despite his scorn for the bourgeoisie, he feels compelled to live in their midst due to a feeling of nostalgia for his bourgeois childhood. Harry talks of his admiration for a spotlessly maintained araucaria plant that sits in the stairwell of his lodging house. He sees the plant as a window into this bourgeois world that he feels now excludes him. When Harry recalls his youth, he remembers not a life of bourgeois mediocrity, but fre-

SUMMARY & ANALYSIS

quent moments of transcendence and radiant, meaningful joy. However, these divine incidents have grown increasingly rare over the years, and share nothing at all with the entertainments and occupations absorbing the vast mass of modern people. Feeling hopelessly alienated, Harry says that he is a Steppenwolf: a beast lost in the multitude of human beings, with whom he cannot find happiness or understanding.

At night, in a mood of discontent, Harry goes out to have a drink. As he walks through the rain, he sees over a door in an old stone wall a sign that he has never noticed before. Stepping reluctantly into the muddy street and crossing it, he reads the words "MAGIC THE-ATER—ENTRANCE NOT FOR EVERYBODY—FOR MADMEN ONLY!" in bright letters fleetingly dancing over the wet wall and pavement. The sign disappears without a trace, however, and Harry continues on to have a disgruntled dinner in his usual tavern, the Steel Helmet.

On the way home, however, Harry finds himself back at the wall. He can no longer find a door. A man carrying a tray and a signboard passes by. The signboard reads "ANARCHIST EVENING ENTERTAINMENT—MAGIC THEATER—ENTRANCE NOT FOR EVERY-BODY." This man does not answer Harry's inquiries about the Magic Theater, so Harry attempts to buy an item from his tray. The man hands him a little booklet but leaves before Harry can pay him for it. Having stepped into the mud, Harry heads home with his feet chilly and soaked. When he arrives home, he finds that the booklet, which appears to be the sort of shabby leaflet one might find at a fair, is entitled "Treatise on the Steppenwolf." Fascinated, Harry spends the night reading the treatise, relaying it to us word for word.

The Treatise takes the form of a fable or fairy tale, beginning, "There was once a man, Harry, called the Steppenwolf." It describes Harry's feelings and emotions in extremely precise detail. It calls Harry a Steppenwolf, one whose human and wolfish natures coexist in constant tension. The man-half of the Steppenwolf acts in accordance with normality and respectability, while the wolf-half sees through the absurdity and vanity of such facades. There are moments when Harry's consciousness flows untroubled between wolf and man, and these times provide such miraculous happiness that they illuminate all the other periods of darkness and despair. Yet in all these respects Harry is not alone: many other men have the same conditions of existence, particularly artists and heroes. Such creatures vacillate between the conviction that all of human life is a cruel, bad joke and the belief that man in some way approximates immortal divinity.

Constantly thinking of suicide, Harry finally designates his fiftieth birthday as the day on which he can take his own life. Perversely, the thought of a fixed date gives him a sense of freedom. He looks forward to that day with eagerness, as it signals the end of all his worldly sufferings. According to the Treatise, the Steppenwolf distances himself from the bourgeois class by rejecting its social conventions. Nevertheless, many aspects of his life are thoroughly ordinary. Against this framework, the Steppenwolf can follow either the path of the saint by developing his spirit or the path of a profligate by pursuing sensual pleasures. Unable to choose, the Steppenwolf walks a compromised path between the two. As a result of having cut himself free of all conventional attachment, the Steppenwolf is utterly liberated but also utterly lonely.

According to the Treatise, in order to rescue himself, the Steppenwolf must look into his own soul and know himself. The Treatise then muses cryptically on some future possibilities for the Steppenwolf: that he may come to experience the importance of humor, may "get hold of one of our little mirrors," or may find his way to a "magic theater." After this comprehensive, authoritative description of the Steppenwolf framework, however, the Treatise criticizes it. It calls the notion of a "Steppenwolf" too simplistic, for Harry consists of innumerable souls, not merely two.

With this criticism the Treatise ends. It reminds Harry of a poem he wrote in which he described himself as a wolf. He reflects that he has two representations of himself, one in verse, one in objective prose. Both versions, Harry believes, are correct, and both point to suicide if he cannot find a way to break through and achieve profound change by deep self-understanding.

ANALYSIS

Hesse tells Harry Haller's story from many perspectives in order to heighten its realism. We first learn about Harry through his landlady's nephew, whose observations about Haller seem to give us the objective truth. We then begin to learn about Harry from his own perspective, which gives us access to his inner life. Finally, we learn about Harry through the authoritative dicta of the mysterious, seemingly definitive Treatise. Because the Treatise employs such phrases as "I say," "even the best of us," and "this Steppenwolf of ours," it has a personal feel, suggesting that the Treatise's unknown author has a personal connection to Harry.

Much like a court case, these three sources of information about Harry Haller corroborate each other, lending credence to Harry and his claims. Such corroboration is important since, with the appearance of the Treatise, Steppenwolf introduces the first of its fantastic, supernatural events. Of course, even with the corroboration among different sources, we are not likely to believe everything Harry says about the disappearing entrance to the Magic Theater and the thoroughly biographical booklet. Yet the narrator's preface prepares us for these fantastic elements by stating that, even if not all of its contents are factually true, Harry's manuscript is nonetheless important as a record of a spiritual journey. In this way, the novel's multiple sources neatly comment upon and enrich each other.

Though these different sources support each other, they also come into conflict in certain ways. For example, while the Treatise has a perfect understanding of Harry's Steppenwolf dichotomy, it insists that the dichotomy is incorrect—Harry, like all people, is made up of innumerable selves rather than simply two polar opposites. Thus, after Harry has earnestly portrayed himself as a Steppenwolf torn between the divine and the bestial, the Treatise deconstructs Harry's idea, critiquing it for being too simplistic. This lesson is furthered by the fact that the text itself reflects the principle of multiple selves. The very structure of the novel imitates this concept of the divided self by breaking itself up into the perspectives of several narrators. The split between Harry's personal record and the objective Treatise mirrors the split that the Steppenwolf experiences in his own life.

The power of this section comes partly from the symbolic opposition set up in the preface, when Harry reads the passage about the divide between life on solid ground (symbolizing the life of the bourgeois) and the stormy, unsteady life of water (symbolizing Harry's own life). The water symbolism suggests that Harry is moving away from the safety and security of the bourgeois. Harry sees the sign announcing the Magic Theater reflected on the wet streets. In addition, he is not able to read the sign until he crosses the street, which he has been reluctant to do because it is wet and muddy. Afterward, Harry describes himself as having stepped squarely into the mud, and he points out that his feet are thoroughly wet and cold.

These persistent references to water and wetness are consistent with the dichotomy of the quote in the preface. Stepping off the solid earth of the pavement—literally getting his feet wet—indicates Harry's shift into deeper, more dangerous territory. Moreover, the image of water evokes ideas of uncertain suspension, imminent dissolution of the self, the danger of drowning, and even the potential for a total drenching of the senses—associative meanings that foreshadow the actions and patterns of the rest of the novel.

THE SECOND PART OF HARRY HALLER'S RECORDS

After the "Treatise on the Steppenwolf" through the meeting with Hermine

SUMMARY

After closing the Treatise and reading his own poem about the Steppenwolf, Harry reflects on what the Treatise predicts for his future. Harry's idea that he will kill himself unless he goes through a profound change reminds him of other instances in his life when ego-shattering experiences led to better and stronger spiritual growth. He recalls two such instances and the terrible times that followed them: the loss of his career and being chased out by his wife. Despite the fact that these turbulent events ultimately had positive consequences, Harry begins to feel too weak to undergo another painful period. He feels he would rather commit suicide than face the prospect of such horrible agony. In fact, the idea of committing suicide on his fiftieth birthday—as chosen by the Steppenwolf of the Treatise—seems too far off, a full two years away.

The following day, Harry concludes that the Treatise is clever and well written but still too general to capture his own unique situation. He is again wracked by anguish and isolation, and he searches in vain for the entrance to the Magic Theater and the signboard man who gave him the Treatise. Harry searches for some time but finds nothing. One day, following a whim, he joins a funeral procession, and one of the men in the procession seems to be the man with the signboard. Harry asks this man where the show will be that night. The man does not recognize Harry but tells him to go to the Black Eagle if he's looking for a show.

Harry runs into a professor, a former colleague of his, who invites him over for dinner. Harry is initially very grateful for this instance of human warmth, but later, as he gets ready to leave for the professor's house, he resents the impending social niceties. At the professor's, Harry's frustration at the misery of having to pretend to share the solid, upstanding life of the professor and his wife gets the better of him. Harry ruins the evening by dramatically insulting a portrait of Goethe, the celebrated German poet, which hangs in the professor's living room. Harry perceives that the portrait is pompous, which deeply offends the professor's wife. Instead of apologizing, Harry makes a clean sweep and confesses to the professor his utter opposition to the man's way of life.

Harry realizes the night has been a total victory for his wolf-half, as he feels he has irreparably severed the very last of his ties to humanity. Shamed and furious with himself, Harry concludes that there is no other option but to end his life. He starts to feel afraid of death, however, and flees from the idea. Paralyzed and dreading the prospect of returning to his rented room, where he believes he will commit suicide, Harry wanders through the city for hours until he finds himself at a public house called the Black Eagle. At its bar, he meets a "pale and pretty girl," who asks him his name. Harry begins to confess much of his situation. The girl makes him clean his glasses, orders him something to eat and drink, and mocks his dirty shoes. She calls Harry a baby when she learns that although he claims that he has taken great trouble to live life, he has never bothered to learn to dance.

Harry realizes there is something strangely familiar about this girl. At first, he thinks she reminds him of a childhood love, Rosa Kreisler, but decides that this is not the connection. Harry tells the girl about the Goethe incident, and she tells him he should not have taken the portrait so seriously. She says that it is hypocritical for Harry to think that he alone is allowed to decide what Goethe should really look like, and that the appropriate behavior in the face of such a misguided portrait is to laugh. In fact, she adds, Harry makes her laugh.

Although she is straightforward, direct, and simple in her manner, the girl seems to understand precisely what Harry needs. He is won over by her maternal treatment and wants to obey all her orders. When the girl eventually gets up to dance, Harry panics but then oddly follows her suggestion of falling asleep right there at his table amid the loud noise and merry people. While Harry sleeps he conjures up Goethe in a dream, which he thinks may also be populated by the German authors Matthisson and Bürger, as well as Molly, a character in Bürger's poems. Harry accuses Goethe of propagating a lie by teaching optimism in a life that Goethe knew was filled with despair. But Goethe avoids all of Harry's questions and says Harry takes him too seriously. Goethe claims that the proper attitude is humor and that seriousness is an "accident of time" that stems from placing "too high a value on time." Goethe then plays a trick on Harry by offering him a leg that turns out to be a scorpion.

When Harry wakes, he does not want the girl to leave him. They agree to meet the following Tuesday. Before she leaves, the girl says that she understands how Harry feels about Goethe, that the portrait is an image or icon that reflects not the true nature of the figure it represents but an excessively romanticized false persona. She has felt the same way in front of pictures of the saints. When Harry asks the girl if she is religious, she replies that she was at one time and, though she is not now, she expects to be so again in the future. The girl also says that to be religious, one must have "independence of time." Finally, she solves Harry's worry about returning to his room: she suggests he pass the night in a rented bedroom at the Black Eagle. Harry feels that the kindness and perfect sympathy of this strange girl have redeemed him and saved him from despondency and doom.

Analysis

Though Harry's initial conclusion—that the Treatise is too general to apply to his particular situation—heightens the novel's sense of realism, the girl challenges his rational approach to the world. Harry's skepticism lends the sometimes-fantastic narrative a sense of rationality, making the story seem less like a fairy tale and more like a documentary. However, Harry's skepticism also makes him somewhat blind to the signs and gifts that life providentially bestows upon him. The girl goes so far as to suggest that only by leaving reason behind can Harry combat his depressed, suicidal nature. She challenges his reliance on rationality by pointing out that in his despondence, he has not taken the time to learn to dance. The girl alerts Harry to the pleasures and wonders of the world that are constantly around him but that he never notices.

The wolf-half of Harry first manifests itself when he has difficulty communicating with the professor and the girl in these chapters. Harry is unable to tolerate human compassion, and as a result he denies others' attempts to connect with him. The incident at the professor's home suggests, however, that this process is not entirely

Harry's fault. After all, Harry is surrounded by people who out-wardly seem to resemble him but are actually totally different. The girl, who is from a very different class and upbringing than Harry, illustrates the need to look beyond surface resemblances to find truly complementary people. The girl represents an encounter with the radically different, an encounter that is necessary to incite change in Harry. The Treatise points out this contrast, arguing that we are all made up of innumerable selves. On the surface, Harry and the girl seem to contrast, but because they are each complex people composed of numerous identities, their characters are actu-ally complementary.

As the girl takes responsibility for Harry, her actions take on deep symbolic meaning that suggests her role as a force for change in Harry's life. The girl also proposes that one way Harry will experi-ence change is through the development of his sense of humor. The girl cleans Harry's glasses, symbolizing the newfound clarity with which he begins to evaluate himself. She notices the mud on his shoes, which in its intangibility represents the opposite of the solid-ity of down-to-earth bourgeois existence. The girl also echoes Goethe's statement about time, telling Harry that the best thing to do in the face of the silly mediocrities of the world is merely to laugh. The girl's advice regarding laughter becomes a significant philo-sophical point of the novel. As both the Treatise and Harry's dream of Goethe also address humor, Hesse suggests that humor is a char-acteristic of the enlightened.

This section highlights the disjunction between representation and reality. Harry denigrates the Treatise for not corresponding closely enough to the reality and complexity of his own situation. He also becomes violently perturbed that Goethe's portrait could not possibly be an accurate portrayal of the dead poet. In both cases, the unreality of the representation upsets Harry deeply. We see that Harry and the girl have different points of view with regard to rep-resentation: Harry feels that images have the power to corrupt and distort our perceptions of reality, while the girl points out that rep-resentations should not be taken too seriously and that the power to represent belongs equally to everyone. This argument parallels the argument of the Steppenwolf treatise, which points out that the image of the Steppenwolf is too simplistic to adequately describe Harry. Ultimately, the girl's argument implies that images of the human body are likewise incapable of adequately describing the various personalities that inhabit it.

THE THIRD PART OF HARRY HALLER'S RECORDS

After the Black Eagle through the Tea Dance

SUMMARY

> "Oh! how stiff you are! Just go straight ahead as if
> you were walking . . . Dancing, don't you see, is every
> bit as easy as thinking. . . ."
>
> (See QUOTATIONS, p. 42)

Harry runs into his landlady upon returning to his house the next morning. He feels unusually talkative, and they have a pleasant cup of tea together. Harry comments on ancient Indian philosophy, which he says understands the "unreality of time" that has now only been manifest by the device of the radio. Harry points out his disappointment that modern man uses the radio merely as one of his many distractions. He almost launches into a rant, but he holds back his bitterness and makes a joke instead.

Harry waits impatiently for Tuesday, when he is to have dinner with the girl from the Black Eagle. He views his interactions with the girl as the only way he can change his life and avoid suicide. Tuesday finally comes, and during dinner, the girl's intelligent manner switches between charming jovialness and utter seriousness. Her behavior fascinates Harry. When Harry asks her name, she points out that her face resembles a boy's and asks him to guess. Because the girl reminds Harry of a childhood friend called Herman, he guesses, correctly, that her name is Hermine.

Hermine tells Harry that she is a kind of mirror for him, one that responds to his gaze with understanding. He does indeed see how looking at his "opposite" is like looking into a "magic mirror." Hermine explains that Harry needs her—that he is "dying just for the lack of a push to throw [him] into the water and bring [him] to life again"—and that she is going to teach him how to dance, laugh, and live. She also tells Harry she will fulfill his needs, but in return she will make him fall in love with her and then make him obey a final command: to kill her. Harry accepts without protest. By the end of their talk, he feels that Hermine has seen through him entirely, and he tells her his secret about the Treatise.

Harry and Hermine agree to start dance lessons, and she tells him to buy a gramophone and records. Even though Harry hesitates to immerse himself in the jazz music of the times, which he dislikes, he has agreed to obey all of Hermine's commands. During their meetings, they discuss the Treatise and their daily thoughts. Each time they meet, Hermine displays surprising wisdom, but she always cuts short their conversations with some comment that highlights the uselessness of excessive thought. Once, for example, after a long talk about the inevitability of war, Hermine points out the value of living and seizing life, even if only for a short time. Later, she suggests that Harry's lack of engagement with life is just as problematic as others' lack of engagement with serious thought. Hermine, on the other hand, is able to enjoy even the smallest tasks of daily existence, such as choosing a gramophone or pulling meat off a duck bone.

After two foxtrot lessons, Hermine takes Harry to a restaurant, which he sees as a world of unintelligent, unthinking pleasure-seekers. There, after a few dances together, Hermine encourages Harry to overcome his shyness and ask a pretty blonde to dance with him. He does so despite his belief that he is a stiff old man and his fear that he will be laughed at. The girl, who he later learns is called Maria, accepts. Maria's own effortless grace makes Harry feel like this is the first time he has really danced.

At the dance, Harry also meets Pablo, a striking but taciturn young bandleader who Hermine claims "could play on all instruments and talk every language in the world." Hermine is very much attached to Pablo. However, Harry is not much impressed as he watches Pablo play his two saxophones and attempts to communicate with the less-than-talkative young man. In the end, Harry dances again with Hermine, and he feels that she is his "double," resembling not only himself but also Herman, his boyhood friend, "the enthusiast, the poet." As they dance, Hermine explains that she suffers exactly the way Harry does in the disappointing, crude world.

ANALYSIS

Steppenwolf recounts Harry's spiritual education and development, and in this section we begin to see Harry's gradual process of change. His encounter with his landlady demonstrates how much he has learned from his night at the Black Eagle. Not only has Harry has become open to human intercourse, but he has also begun to appreciate humor. Instead of going off on a rant about the poverty of modern culture, he manages to make a joke instead. In doing so,

Harry is acting on the lessons that his various mentors in the novel—Hermine and, in his dream, Goethe—have tried to teach him about the efficacy of laughter. Harry has also begun to reflect on the unreality of time. In Harry's dream, Goethe says that seriousness is a result of placing too high a value on time. Later, Hermine points to the possibility of a kind of time outside the constraints of the temporal, lived-in world. Harry's character develops as he begins to assimilate the new arguments and ideas to which he is exposed.

Hermine is both Harry's opposite and his double. Her name is a feminized version of Hermann Hesse's and also sounds similar to Harry's. Hermine's remarks that she looks like a boy and that she is Harry's mirror suggest that her character reflects Harry's own. At the same time, Hermine's interest in the sensual aspects of the world is quite different from Harry's own obsession with morose, contemplative thought. Whereas he is a lonely intellectual and a reactionary against modern popular culture, she embraces everything about life, even its most mundane events. Hermine is well versed in the arts of living and the pleasures of the senses; over time, she teaches Harry the dance of life. Like a mirror image, Hermine seems intangible and almost nonexistent. The fact that she knows so much about Harry, devotes herself so completely to his improvement, and discusses so little of her personal history suggests that she might be an apparition conjured up by Harry's mind to deal with his mental stress.

The fact that Hermine teaches Harry to dance is significant, as Hesse's writings frequently treat music as the most elevated, most divine engagement of humanity. The description of Harry's experience at the symphony in the preface demonstrates how music can serve as a means of transportation into transcendence. Likewise, the image of Pablo playing effortlessly on his two saxophones echoes Harry's earlier mention of the ability to flow untroubled between his wolf-half and man-half. Hermine thus decides to teach Harry how to make his own actions fit in time and tune with music. Dancing requires human interaction, furthering the suggestion that Hermine is Harry's partner or double. Hesse is deeply concerned with the problem of a divided or splintered self, so the image of two people moving as though they were one resonates strongly with the novel's philosophical concerns.

Though Hesse was greatly influenced by the German Romantics, *Steppenwolf* does not follow the stylistic conventions of German Romanticism. Rather than setting his novel in a stylized world in which the supernatural and unnatural take place, Hesse draws the magical out of the everyday. He grounds his novel in the world of the mundane, the recognizable, and the common. As a result, Harry's experience with Hermine is rife with worldly details: shopping for a gramophone, buying records, and learning the popular dance steps of the day. Hesse's own writing echoes Harry's experience: just as Harry allows popular music to infiltrate his jealously guarded intellectual lifestyle to come to a real engagement with life, Hesse writes on a mundane and contemporary plane to approach something more transcendent.

THE FOURTH PART OF HARRY HALLER'S RECORDS

Pablo and Maria

SUMMARY

Harry's immersion in the world of dancing, drink, nightclubs, and restaurants is accompanied by what he calls a "disintegration of the personality." In keeping with the principles set out in the Treatise, Harry starts to see himself as a composite of thousands of other souls. This disintegration is very painful, especially when these selves jar and come into conflict, which makes Harry feel that he is defiling everything he has held sacred in his life. At the same time, though, Harry is able to see for the first time the blind hypocrisy of his former life. He has been in his own way just as pompous and one-sided as the portrait of Goethe he earlier condemned.

Harry spends a considerable amount of time in the company of Pablo. He tells Pablo about his musical theories, but the response he receives is always a quiet, smiling indifference, which frustrates him. When Harry is particularly annoyed by one such exchange, Pablo offers him a pinch from his gold snuffbox, and Harry sniffs a cocaine-laced powder. One day, Harry finally manages to engage Pablo in a discussion, but Pablo responds to all of Harry's theoretical discourse by saying that music has nothing to do with good taste, right, wrong, or education. Instead, music is about creating as much, as well, and as intensely as possible. Harry tries to defend higher, spiritual music, but he cannot argue against Pablo's firm belief that music is made first and foremost to give pleasure.

One night, Harry is feeling particularly upset about his newfound hedonism. He is practically on the verge of cursing Hermine and going back to his original plan to commit suicide. However, when he enters his room he finds that the beautiful Maria is lying in his bed. Maria has arrived at Hermine's request, and Hermine wants Harry to make love to Maria. That night, Harry sleeps with Maria.

Rather than feeling that Maria defiles his spirituality, Harry finds that she is its "worthy fulfillment." The next day, he rents a room in a nearby neighborhood for their amorous meetings. Even though Harry is not Maria's only lover, he is drunk with the sensual delights she provides. Being with her is the first time since his downfall that he has been excited about his life. Through the feeling Maria kindles in him, and through all the sensual arts she teaches him, Harry recalls all the romantic affairs of his life, as well as all the friendships. He realizes that these experiences constitute his life's wealth.

Harry learns more about Maria and Hermine's life of champagne, drugs, and wealthy men. He also learns about the accoutrements of love affairs and about the small gifts that lovers give each other. Like Hermine, Maria is infatuated with the young Pablo, who is apparently another of her lovers. In fact, at one point Pablo suggests that the three of them have an ménage à trois, but Harry vigorously objects. Another time, Pablo asks Harry for money, suggesting, to Harry's horror, that he take that night with Maria in exchange.

In the three weeks preceding the annual Fancy Dress Ball organized by the Society of Artists, Harry continues to feel connected to Hermine, who understands him well. On the day before the ball, she comes to his apartment, and they have a long, intense talk. Harry explains that although he has been happy with Maria, he does not feel right about the happiness because it does not lead anywhere and because he is not made for such contentment. What Harry really wants is to suffer beautifully and long for death. Hermine understands Harry and explains that for him, as for her, life has not asked the great sacrifices and achievements they are both prepared to make. Instead it has offered a gaudy whirl of stupid, ephemeral tricks. Hermine says that the two of them are among those who suffer because they have a "dimension too many," and she speaks of a kingdom of "eternity" that exists after death, a kingdom to which all of the geniuses and saints and heroes of history belong.

Inspired by Hermine's words, Harry writes a poem about the perfect, unchanging "immortals." He is amazed that Hermine has managed to understand his deepest, half-conscious sentiments so well. He feels that she understands him almost too well. Harry even begins to suspect that she has somehow drawn the feelings out of

him. He spends the night before the ball with Maria, who has a pre-
monition that this is the last time they will be together. Harry sus-
pects that Hermine will claim him at the ball.

ANALYSIS

As the Treatise has claimed, Harry gradually begins to discover that
he has many souls or identities. During the period when Hermine
teaches him to dance and Maria teaches him to love, Harry develops
the various personalities that lie latent within each person. He himself begins to see his so-called soul as an ever-growing collection of
souls. Harry's increasing intimacy with Pablo and Maria in the
external world is symbolic of the internal development he is under-
going, creating multiple internal parts of himself. Yet Harry senses
that this proliferation is not an end in itself: the generation of
Harry's many different parts has accomplished the job of breaking
the stereotype of the Steppenwolf. However, it remains to be seen
how the Steppenwolf is taught to accept all of these parts, and how
it is taught to laugh.

One way to interpret *Steppenwolf* is to dismiss the magic quali-
ties of its odd happenings and credit them instead to the heated,
insistent imagination of a desperate, teetering, aging man. Harry's
response to Maria is sudden and total; he had previously been so
focused on books and music that sexual experience is completely
foreign and mysterious to him. The account of Harry's love affair
with Maria can come across as sincere and touching, but it can also
seem terribly embarrassing. When they dance and make love, Harry
is very conscious and shy about the fact that he is an old man, and he
cannot imagine why a beautiful girl like Maria would choose to
have anything to do with him. Harry's concern suggests the possibility that all of his distaste for society is a result of his insecurity about
his age. After all, until Harry meets Hermine, the story of the Steppenwolf is just a document of social debacle after social debacle.

Hesse likely intends the reader to sympathize with Harry's infat-
uation, however. Deeply influenced by Asian philosophy, Hesse's
brand of mystical symbolism embraced both spiritual and physical
aspects of human life. Maria is a total incarnation of the physical,
sensual sphere. Some critics have pointed out the reductive simplic-
ity of this opposition between physical and spiritual life, accusing
Hesse of chauvinism for using a woman as a representative of anti-
intellectualism. Despite Hesse's best attempts to credit Maria with

being wise in her own ways—the ways of love—she often comes across as false and forced. As a result, when Hermine discusses the suffering that belongs to those with "a dimension too many," we are left with the uncomfortable suspicion that she lacks an adequate understanding of the true complexities of other people. Whatever the case, we can see that by the Fancy Dress Ball Harry has made up his mind: the only two options for people like him are a life of beautiful suffering or a noble, paradoxically immortal death.

THE FIFTH PART OF HARRY HALLER'S RECORDS

The Fancy Dress Ball

SUMMARY

> *An experience fell to my lot . . . that I had never known . . . the mystic union of joy.*
> (See QUOTATIONS, p. 43)

Harry plans to meet Hermine at the Fancy Dress Ball, which is a masquerade. He is going without a costume, while she is going in a costume she has not revealed to him. That night, Harry goes to his old haunt, the Steel Helmet, for dinner. He is filled with a sense of nostalgia for his former life, and also a sense that he is bidding it farewell. He reflects on the lamentable nature of modernity. Harry considers himself to be neither old-fashioned nor of the present day, believing he has "escaped time altogether." Since it is still too early for him to go to the ball, on a whim he stops off at a cinema and watches part of the Old Testament on-screen.

Once at the masked ball, Harry is immediately swept up in the swirl of festivities. Each part of the Globe Rooms is given over to the ball, with dancing in every room, even the basement. Everyone at the party is in a good mood except Harry, who is surly and aloof because he cannot find Hermine or Maria anywhere. He tries to leave, but once at the cloakroom he realizes he has lost the ticket for his coat. A stranger whisks by and gives Harry his own ticket, upon which are scrawled the words "TONIGHT AT THE MAGIC THEATER— FOR MADMEN ONLY—PRICE OF ADMITTANCE YOUR MIND.—NOT FOR EVERYBODY.—HERMINE IS IN HELL."

Harry hurries away to find Hermine, exhilarated once again. Maria, in disguise as a Spanish dancing girl, throws herself into

Harry's arms. As Pablo leads the band, Harry and Maria dance and kiss, but she bids him farewell when she learns that Hermine has summoned him. In the room at the party designated as "hell," Harry sits down at the bar next to a young fellow who turns out to be Hermine disguised as Harry's childhood friend Herman. Talking and drinking champagne, Harry easily falls in love with Hermine, as she had said at their first dinner that he would.

Harry and Hermine break apart to dance with other women, sometimes rivaling each other for the same woman. Harry loses himself in the fairy-tale magic of the ball. For the very first time in his life, he experiences the sense of absorption in a large crowd, the utter dissolution of the self in the collective community that is usually only experienced by students and revelers. Harry feels himself Pablo's brother, innocent and released as a child. He notes that he has "lost the sense of time."

Harry is drawn to a woman in a black Pierrette costume with a white face. He dances with her, and when they kiss, he recognizes that she is Hermine in a new disguise. They dance a climactic "nuptial dance." As the dawn approaches, Harry twice hears an eerie distant laughter from above. Pablo, who has been in another room, appears and invites both Harry and Hermine to a little entertainment, "[f]or madmen only," with only one price: Harry's mind. In a little room bathed in blue light, the three of them smoke Pablo's strange cigarettes and drink an unfamiliar liquid, which packs an immediate punch. Pablo, for the first time articulate and voluble, explains that Harry has always desired to penetrate to that realm beyond time, but that this world beyond time exists only in his own soul. Pablo says that he is now going to make this world of Harry's soul visible.

SUMMARY & ANALYSIS

ANALYSIS

In this section Hesse develops the idea of escaping time. First suggested by Goethe in Harry's dream and echoed by Hermine just before the Fancy Dress Ball, the idea of being beyond time again comes to Harry through a feeling he has during his visit to the Steel Helmet. Harry reiterates this sentiment at the height of his revelry at the ball, where Pablo, as he prepares Harry for the Magic Theater, reinforces it yet again. Although clearly an important theme in *Steppenwolf*, the idea of escaping time remains vague and not entirely consistent. On the one hand, the theme is connected with the recurrent motif of the immortals, geniuses such as Goethe and Mozart who inhabit the space of eternity. In her talk with Harry before the ball, Hermine speaks of the world beyond time as the place for which she and Harry—those "with a dimension too many"—are destined, ostensibly after death. But when Pablo discusses the idea of a realm beyond time, he links it with the world of Harry's soul. The novel suggests that the world of eternity exists as a possibility only when we die, yet also implies that it is a realm of transcendence we carry within us.

We see Harry's dramatic change from an ascetic intellectual to a passionate hedonist in the changing way he relates to a crowd. Harry's momentary disgust with the wild, crude merrymaking around him demonstrates the extent of his change. It is only Hermine's intervention that enables Harry to merge with the crowd, becoming one with them in a communal frenzy and fervor.

Harry likens the release he feels when he merges with the crowd to the innocence of a child. Hesse draws this idea—the child as symbolic of sensual pleasures—from the theoretical systems of the nineteenth-century German thinkers Friedrich Nietzsche and Emile Durkheim. Nietzsche's famous work *Thus Spake Zarathustra* sets up a three-part categorization of the spiritual evolution of individuals: the third and final stage is that of a child, whose role is to say the "sacred yes" in innocence and wisdom. Durkheim's *The Elementary Forms of the Religious Life* identifies a very important mode of social behavior, the carnival, in which all restrictions are overturned for a specified time; the carnival serves as a release valve for a society's pent-up, repressed energy. Durkheim notes the feeling of "collective effervescence" that occurs when the individual at such a gathering feels submerged in a state of union with the larger social mass—exactly the feeling Harry has at the climax of the ball. Just as it conforms to elements of Durkheim's analysis, Harry's dissolution in the larger mass signals that he has learned the lessons of the Treatise and shattered his sense of himself as a singular unit into a thousand different souls.

As Harry becomes increasingly similar to Hermine, it becomes clear that she is nearing the end of her project of teaching him. Harry will soon have to kill Hermine according to their original agreement. This situation strongly suggests that that Hermine is not real but only a reflection of some part of Harry's self. Hermine's appearance at the ball—so well disguised as "Herman" that Harry does not even recognize her—foreshadows her eventual disappearance.

Harry has described Herman as a boyhood friend, a poet of ecstasy and transcendence, without ever mentioning what happened to Herman or how such a close friend fell out of his life. By now, we sense that "Herman" actually represents the innocent, pure, life-loving part of Harry that has been buried and warped by so many damaging years. Arriving at the ball in the guise of "Herman," Hermine unmasks herself as a fiction of Harry's inner self. Hermine unmasks herself because she is no longer needed; once recognized as part of Harry, the only possible next step is for her to disappear.

THE SIXTH PART OF HARRY HALLER'S RECORDS

The Magic Theater

SUMMARY

> *"Nothing," said he in the mirror, "I am only waiting. I am waiting for death."*
> *"Where is death then?"*
> *"Coming," said the other.*
>
> (See QUOTATIONS, p. 44)

Outside the Magic Theater, Pablo holds a small looking glass up to Harry. Harry sees the trembling reflection of a creature into which a man and wolf flow irregularly, each trying to destroy the other. Harry recognizes that this is how he sees himself, and that with Pablo's help all of his soul will be made visible to him. Pablo leads Harry and Hermine into a horseshoe-shaped theater. He explains that victory over time is achieved through the dissolution of the personality. Pablo instructs Harry to walk down the left corridor while Hermine walks down the right. He shows Harry the pocket mirror again and tells him that the Magic Theater is a "school of humor." Harry laughs, fully and with a feeling of wonderful release. The mirror chars, as though burned, and turns opaque.

Congratulating Harry and laughing the same eerie laugh from the end of the dance, Pablo tells Harry that the Magic Theater is a world of "pictures, not realities." To cast aside the "spectacles" of his old personality, Harry looks into a gigantic mirror in which he sees infinite Harrys of all ages. One is a young teen who leaps out and runs down the corridor. Harry runs after the teen and stops with him at a door that reads "ALL GIRLS ARE YOURS — ONE QUARTER IN

THE SLOT." The boy disappears into the slot. Harry discovers everyone else has also disappeared, and he is left to negotiate the Magic Theater alone.

Harry opens a door that reads "JOLLY HUNTING — GREAT HUNT IN AUTOMOBILES." He finds himself in the middle of a war between men and machines. The scene is apocalyptic, filled with flames and death and reckless, gratuitous bloodshed. Gustav, Harry's school friend, suddenly appears. Next, Harry opens a door that bears the words "GUIDANCE IN THE BUILDING UP OF THE PERSONALITY. SUCCESS GUARANTEED." Inside, a man who looks like Pablo asks Harry to put the pieces of his personality on a chessboard, and shows him how to infinitely reconfigure them. When finished, Harry puts these wonderful pieces into his pocket.

The third door Harry chooses is marked "MARVELOUS TAMING OF THE STEPPENWOLF." Inside, Harry watches a man humiliate a broken wolf by making it behave like a man. Harry is horrified to see the hungry wolf swallow chocolate while it is forced to put its paws around a rabbit and a lamb. Then man and wolf switch positions, and the man rips off his clothes and tears through the flesh of the rabbit and lamb as if he were a beast. In the fourth room Harry enters, "ALL GIRLS ARE YOURS," he gets to enjoy all the women he has ever wanted in his life. Each one of these lovers readies him for his final encounter with Hermine.

Finally, Harry stands in front of a door marked "HOW ONE KILLS FOR LOVE." He is reminded of his early conversation with Hermine, when she told him she would give him a final command to kill her. Filled with dread, Harry reaches in his pockets for the pieces of his life so that he may rework them into a different conclusion. However, all he manages to fish out of his pocket is a knife. Harry runs away, back to the gigantic mirror, where he sees a wolf that turns into Harry. The reflection tells Harry that it is waiting for death.

Strains of the opera *Don Giovanni* and a peal of unearthly laughter herald the appearance of the composer Mozart, the person Harry most admires. The two discuss music and see Brahms and Wagner marching drearily below past them, dragging hosts of followers. Mozart does a somersault and laughs at Harry for being so despondent. Harry tries to catch Mozart's pigtail, but it turns into the tail of a comet, which Harry follows into the cold atmosphere of immortals. Harry then passes out.

When he comes to, Harry returns to the final door. He opens it to see Hermine and Pablo sleeping on the floor naked. Harry immediately thrusts the knife under Hermine's left breast, the spot where Pablo has left a mark. Pablo awakes, smiles, hides Hermine's wound with a corner of the rug, and leaves. Mozart enters, now in modern dress, and begins fixing a radio set. When Mozart turns on the radio, Harry is horrified that Mozart has sided with this terrible, modern, and mediocre bourgeois machine. Mozart laughs, explaining that the radio displays the battle between the real and the ideal, between humanity and divinity. Criticizing Harry for having done such a foolish thing as to kill Hermine, Mozart sends Harry to "HARRY'S EXECUTION." In a bare yard enclosed by four walls, Harry is indicted for misusing the Magic Theater and for having no humor. A frightening, otherworldly laughter descends upon him.

Harry comes to again, and Mozart is there to tell him that he cannot die. He says that Harry must live on to "listen to the cursed radio music of life" and that he must go on to "live and to learn to laugh." When Harry threatens refusal, Mozart offers Harry a cigarette and suddenly transforms into Pablo. Pablo, referring to Hermine, is disappointed that Harry has made such a mess of the Magic Theater. Pablo picks up Hermine, who shrinks into a toy figure, and packs her into his waistcoat pocket. Pablo tells Harry that he will do better the next time.

At this point, Harry understands everything. He understands that "all the hundred thousand pieces of life's game were in [his] pocket," and he is determined to start the game anew. The novel closes with the optimistic words: "One day I would be a better hand at the game. One day I would learn how to laugh. Pablo was waiting for me, and Mozart too."

> *I understood it all . . . . I knew that all the hundred thousand pieces of life's game were in my pocket.*
> (See QUOTATIONS, p.45)

ANALYSIS: THE MAGIC THEATER

The episode of the Magic Theater questions the boundary between life and art. The worlds Harry discovers inside the doors are highly stylized representations that match up to an emotional or psychic reality rather than depicting a physical reality. They remind us of theatrical arts as well as visual ones: Harry is in a theater, and his actions are actually a performance. Pablo himself declares that the Magic Theater is a place of pictures rather than reality. We are entirely in the realm of art or magic. Critic Ralph Freedman suggests that the scenes behind the doors symbolize the transformation of life into art, and that the mirror of art transforms what is ambivalent in real life into images and motifs. Freedman argues that Hesse's sense of being both wanted and rejected is manifest in Harry's "pilgrimage among alternating motifs: those depicting pleasure, a unified vision, humor, or transcendence contrasted with others which depict isolation, failure, betrayal, and despair."

The Magic Theater scene clarifies the importance of laughter, one of the novel's key concerns. From the start, Pablo explains that the Magic Theater is a school of humor. Pablo laughs constantly and encourages Harry to laugh at his own personality and life. When Harry encounters Mozart, the composer also states that Harry takes life too seriously, and he laughs the beautiful laughter of the immortals. In this regard, Mozart resembles the jocund Goethe of Harry's dream at the Black Eagle.

The nature of the laughter that these characters discuss, however, is complex. It is not the kind of laughter that results from a propensity to see the sunny side of life. Rather, in *Steppenwolf* laughter is seen as a response not to the amusing but to the dreadful. The laughter of the immortals belongs to them because it transcends the dramas and worries of human life. Though Harry does not learn the lessons of the school of humor right away, at the end of the novel he optimistically believes that he will.

Harry's determination to try to learn how to laugh suggests that a great, transcendent life is not out of mortal reach. Indeed, in much of the Magic Theater episode, Hesse laughs at his own writing in the same way that his characters suggest Harry should laugh at his life. Hesse's painfully earnest story of a tortured, gifted man may make the author seem humorless. But there is a strong element of self-mockery in the Magic Theater episode that reveals Hesse's sense of humor.

Hesse's self-mockery is most obvious in the embedded titles of some of the doors in the Magic Theater. Doors along the corridor promise things such as "delightful suicide," "the wisdom of the East," "transformation from time into space by means of music," "downfall of the West," "laughing tears," and "solitude made easy." These titles are a catalog of Hesse's own obsessions, the ideas that appear throughout *Steppenwolf* and Hesse's other works. That Hesse can list his obsessions so plainly shows that he is fully aware of his own inclinations. Furthermore, the fact that Hesse reduces his obsessions to unceremonious phrases, thrown out helter-skelter in the fantastic Magic Theater, is an indication that he can laugh at them, that he does not take them too seriously. The door titles imply subtly that Hesse has arrived at a fuller reconciliation of his own multiple selves and has learned the lesson of humor that Harry glimpses at the novel's conclusion.

IMPORTANT QUOTATIONS
EXPLAINED

1. He went on two legs, wore clothes and was a human
    being, but nevertheless he was in reality a wolf of the
    Steppes. He had learned a good deal . . . and was a
    fairly clever fellow. What he had not learned, however,
    was this: to find contentment in himself and his own
    life. The cause of this apparently was that at the
    bottom of his heart he knew all the time (or thought
    he knew) that he was in reality not a man, but a wolf
    of the Steppes.

These are the opening lines of the "Treatise on the Steppenwolf," a
work that describes minutely the psychological condition of a
man, Harry Haller, who harbors two souls within him. One soul is
that of an ordinary man interested in the ordinary aspects of
human life. The other—his truer, deeper self—is a wild, cruel wolf
of the steppes. By this point in *Steppenwolf,* the same tormented
half-wolf, half-man characterization has already been put forward
from two other points of view: from Harry's own claims and from
those of his landlady's nephew in the preface. Now, these impossibly accurate opening lines of the Treatise provide a corroboration
of Harry's central conflict, while introducing the first hints that the
novel is not realistic.

In addition, by providing another perspective from which we
may view Harry, the Treatise reflects on a formal level the multiple
selves that exist within the single individual the Treatise describes.
For a work such as *Steppenwolf,* which has complex theoretical
content, the technique of such a Treatise is a very effective invention.
It enables Hesse to lay out his beliefs about the nature of the soul in
a straightforward, didactic fashion.

2.   "Oh! how stiff you are! Just go straight ahead as if
      you were walking . . . Dancing, don't you see, is every
      bit as easy as thinking, when you can do it, and much
      easier to learn. Now you can understand why people
      won't get the habit of thinking. . . ."

Hermine speaks these lines to Harry at their first dance lesson.
Harry has never bothered to learn how to dance and is an utter
beginner, while Hermine, a frequenter of restaurants and nightclubs, is well versed in all the newest steps. Below the surface, however, dance is a stand-in for the compatibility between the life of the
body and the life of the spirit or intellect. By dancing, Harry is tuning his physical actions to the promptings of the divine, which are
symbolized by music.

     All his life Harry has focused on the life of the mind, to the egre-
gious neglect of his body. Alluding to a conversation they have just
had, in which Harry has complained about people who do not
bother themselves to think, Hermine accuses Harry of being just as
lazy and bullheaded as those people he disdains. Over the course of
the novel, Hermine succeeds in motivating Harry to get in touch
with and take pleasure in exerting his more sensuous side. In fact,
Hermine can be seen as a reflection of this lost, repressed part
within Harry—so much so that once he has fully integrated the sensuous and material within himself, he no longer needs her and puts
an end to her.

3. An experience fell to my lot this night of the Ball that I had never known in all my fifty years, though it is known to every flapper and student—the intoxication of a general festivity, the mysterious merging of the personality in the mass, the mystic union of joy.

This passage appears during the climactic Fancy Dress Ball, where Harry and Hermine dance with innumerable partners and relish the wild revelry to the fullest. Harry's experience of blending with the community and feeling his personality dissolve into the collective mass represents the culmination of everything that Hermine and others have been trying to teach him. Harry's absorption of the key lesson about the multifaceted nature of the soul has taken place, through the path of the body and through the kind of modern frivolities that Harry has spent a lifetime disdaining. Furthermore, these truths and this path do not belong to Harry alone but are properties and potentialities of people in general. Indeed, by realizing that his triumph is a common one, "known to every flapper and student," Harry breaks the egotistical notion that he is specially gifted or destined. This final break with his previous insistence on the self enables Harry's merging into the mass of people.

4. Again I looked into the mirror. I had been mad. I must have been mad. There was no wolf in the mirror, lolling his tongue in his maw. It was I, Harry. . . . My face was gray, forsaken of all fancies, wearied by all vice, horribly pale. Still it was a human being, someone one could speak to.
"Harry," I said, "what are you doing there?"
"Nothing," said he in the mirror, "I am only waiting. I am waiting for death."
"Where is death then?"
"Coming," said the other.

This passage, part of the climactic episode at the novel's close in Pablo's Magic Theater, touches on many of the novel's themes and motifs. It addresses the concept of mirrors with semi-independent reflections, Harry's inclination toward death, Mozart and unearthly music, and the beyond-world of immortal genius. Finally, the passage alludes to the divide between wolf and man within Harry, and refers to the ideas of to vice and madness. On a formal level, this passage exemplifies the most memorable technique Hesse uses in *Steppenwolf*: an eerie, surreal, fantasy-world encounter that serves as a visible manifestation, a hallucinatory correlative, for Harry's internal state. These flights of brilliant fantasy are what make Hesse's didactic concerns and obsessions palatable, and this passage demonstrates Hesse at his most characteristically unique.

5.   I understood it all. I understood Pablo. I understood
      Mozart, and somewhere behind me I heard his ghastly
      laughter. I knew that all the hundred thousand pieces
      of life's game were in my pocket . . . I would traverse
      not once more, but often, the hell of my inner being.
      One day I would be a better hand at the game. One
      day I would learn how to laugh. Pablo was waiting for
      me, and Mozart too.

These are the final lines of the novel. Pablo has just packed up his
hallucinatory Magic Theater, including the slain Hermine, who
shrinks to the size of a figurine. Pablo has also informed Harry
that although he has failed this time, he will no doubt perform better on a future visit. As we see here, Harry instantly comprehends
the meaning of the Magic Theater—of Pablo, of laughter, of the
pieces of his personality. Whether we as readers have "understood
it all" is another matter. The novel's sudden ending leaves us with a
sense of frustration and suspense. Harry declares that he understands, but his understanding does not help us as readers. If anything is clear, it is that, in Harry's view, Pablo has been elevated to
the status of a wise sage. Part of Harry's newfound respect for
Pablo may be due to his acceptance of Pablo's assertion that laughter is the key to life and insight.

     Our last glimpse of Harry shows him as having failed in the very
instant of his transcendent epiphany. He does not leave the novel a
successful hero. In fact, Harry still looks forward expectantly to
fresh periods of inner hell. Since these periods sound suspiciously
like the periods of despair Harry experiences after first reading the
Treatise, we might wonder what Harry has gained since the beginning of the novel. He has gained understanding, renewed spirit, and
the possession of those tools such as laughter that make it possible
to take up life's challenge.

Key Facts

FULL TITLE
Steppenwolf, or *Der Steppenwolf* (*The Steppenwolf*)

AUTHOR
Hermann Hesse

TYPE OF WORK
Novel

GENRE
Bildungsroman; psychoanalytical adventure

LANGUAGE
German

TIME AND PLACE WRITTEN
Mid-1920s, Switzerland

DATE OF FIRST PUBLICATION
1927

PUBLISHER
S. Fischer

NARRATOR
The novel has multiple narrators: Harry Haller, the protagonist, who has left behind his records; the nephew of Harry's landlady, who composes the preface; and the anonymous, all-knowing author of a booklet called "Treatise on the Steppenwolf."

POINT OF VIEW
The point of view is first person for the vast majority of the novel, though limited third person in the preface by Harry's landlady's nephew, and an all-knowing, omniscient second and third person in the Treatise. All of these points of view take Harry as their focus, and each works in tandem with the others, corroborating and also extending the information given in the other sections.

TONE
The novel's tone varies from direly serious to ironically humorous, at times verging on surreal and eventually hallucinatory.

TENSE
Past

SETTING (TIME)
Between the two world wars

SETTING (PLACE)
An unspecified, medium-sized town in a German-speaking country

PROTAGONIST
Harry Haller, also known as the Steppenwolf

MAJOR CONFLICT
Harry feels divided between two conflicting halves—a man-half who prizes and desires the comforts offered by a respectable life with others, and a wild and cruel wolf-half who scorns such petty concerns. Alienated and despairing, on the verge of suicide at the novel's opening, Harry seeks to resolve the disturbance within him and pick up the task of life again.

RISING ACTION
Harry receives the "Treatise on the Steppenwolf," meets Hermine, has a liaison with Maria, and attends the Fancy Dress Ball.

CLIMAX
During the journey in Pablo's Magic Theater, Harry faces different aspects of himself and kills Hermine, symbolizing his assimilation of his characteristics into his own self-identity.

FALLING ACTION
Harry converses with Mozart.

THEMES
Multiple identities; the existence of a world beyond time; the complex nature of laughter

MOTIFS
Music; dancing; representation

SYMBOLS
Mirrors; the radio; the araucaria plant

FORESHADOWING
The nephew's preface; Hermine's description of her future command

KEY FACTS

STUDY QUESTIONS & ESSAY TOPICS

STUDY QUESTIONS

1. *Why do you suppose Hesse places such emphasis on the Magic Theater? What is the relation between magic and spectacle in the novel, and why should this relation be of interest to Hesse?*

One way of understanding the Magic Theater is as the stage upon which Harry can encounter or give life to all the different manifestations of his personality. Pablo introduces Harry to the Magic Theater by saying that all he will do is make the world of Harry's soul visible. After the self-dramatizing spectacle in the splintering mirrors of the Magic Theater, Harry will be put back together again in a new, rejuvenated configuration.

Magic, magical thinking, and the role of the magician are important in *Steppenwolf*. Magical thinking is a kind of inspired vision that borders on madness, which is why the Magic Theater is advertised as being "for madmen only." Madness and magic involve the ability to arrive at a deeper truth by transcending the material and the everyday. To Hesse, madmen are those who have seen through the morass of social and moral conventions, penetrating to the realm of eternity of the immortals. The figure of the magician is key, because the magician allows a transition into the madness and magic of heightened perception. While Pablo and Hermine are the novel's most obvious magicians, Hesse himself is also such a magician. After all, the power of the author to use symbol and metaphor to give voice and vision to interior life is a kind of analogous magic.

2. *Think of all the ways in which mirrors function in the novel. What significance do they have in the Steppenwolf's quest for himself and the writer's quest for artistic form?*

Reflection is one of the novel's main concerns. The image of the city is reflected in the wet asphalt streets in the opening scene, and as we proceed in the story, reflections and mirrors become increasingly important. Hermine uses a pocket mirror, Harry sees himself and his doubles in mirrors, and the novel climaxes in Pablo's Cabinet of Mirrors, the Magic Theater. In addition, characters also mirror one another: Hermine describes herself as Harry's looking glass. Even the text employs complicated reflections, mirroring both Harry and itself. The "Treatise on the Steppenwolf" is a verbal mirror held up to Harry's psyche, and the editor's preface is echoed by Harry's records, which themselves reflect the words of the Treatise.

Each time a mirror is presented, it does not merely reflect a pure mirror image but corroborates, extends, or draws out other insights. Mirrors are ever-present to remind us of the possibility of double perception, apprehending doubles and opposites at the same moment. This notion of the double or opposite is a useful device for portraying the mind-body split with which Hesse is concerned. Mirrors also raise the question of the writer's role—especially in a novel such as *Steppenwolf,* in which characters such as Harry and Hermine are clearly reflections of the author.

3.   *Using* Steppenwolf *as evidence, why do you think Hesse was so popular with the hippie counterculture of 1960s America?*

Hesse's novels, particularly *Steppenwolf*, resonate with groups of people who find themselves struggling against a system to which they feel they do not belong. As the landlady's nephew expresses in the preface, Harry's illness is not "the eccentricity of a single individual," but instead the illness of the era itself, a "neurosis" of Harry's generation. It is not surprising, then, that the hippies, who felt the stress of the cultural crisis in the 1960s, saw Hesse as a countercultural sage. A key figure in the movement, Timothy Leary, called Hesse his hero and encouraged his followers to read him—especially the Magic Theater segment of *Steppenwolf*, which Leary called a "priceless manual"—before embarking on a hallucinogenic LSD trip. Evidently, Leary felt that he and Hesse had the same mission to achieve a "transpersonal, unitary consciousness."

SUGGESTED ESSAY TOPICS

1. The critic Eugene Stelzig calls Harry Haller the "Hessean psychonaut par excellence." The image of the Steppenwolf as a voyager of the inner world is an apt one. How do the spaces through which Haller physically travels in the novel match the psychic stages through which he passes? (Consider, for example, the bourgeois space of the landlady's lodging house in contrast to the subterranean dens of dancers and musicians.)

2. How are we to understand the character of Hermine? Is she a mother, a friend, a sister, a lover, or every one of those things? What is her significance in relation to Harry? Is she an other, or a part of the same?

3. At the Fancy Dress Ball, Harry considers that the event is "all a fairy tale," "fanciful and symbolic," and endowed with "a new dimension, a deeper meaning." In what ways does *Steppenwolf* conform to the structure and logic of a traditional fairy tale, and in what ways does it not?

4. From what we know of Hesse's background and history, much of *Steppenwolf* clearly stems from real events in his life. What are the implications of this for the novel? Does it alter our sense of *Steppenwolf*'s genre? How does the confessional nature of the work influence our reception of it?

5. By the end of the novel, Harry has learned to approach the modern world with humor, though not with acceptance and contentment. Do you think his earlier concerns and criticisms have been borne out in the intervening years? What aspects of the second half of the twentieth century do you think Harry—or Hesse—would have felt most conformed to his predictions?

QUESTIONS & ESSAYS

REVIEW & RESOURCES

QUIZ

1. Who is the fictional editor who writes the preface to Harry Haller's records?

    A. Harry's old colleague, a professor of Oriental mysticism
    B. Harry's childhood best friend, Herman
    C. Harry's landlady's nephew
    D. Harry's typesetter, Dora

2. What is the first thing the Steppenwolf does when he enters his future landlady's house?

    A. He insults her
    B. He introduces himself
    C. He heaves a weary sigh
    D. He sniffs the air

3. Why is Harry sitting on the landing between the first and second floors of his building?

    A. He is winded from climbing because of his poor health and limping gait
    B. He is mesmerized by the condition of a well-kept plant
    C. He is filled with dread at the thought of returning to his room
    D. He does not want to wake the landlady with his footsteps

4. What is the price of admission to the Magic Theater?

    A. One's mind
    B. One's soul
    C. One's life
    D. One's gender

5. According to the "Treatise on the Steppenwolf," what is the Steppenwolf's given name?

    A. It is nameless
    B. Everyman
    C. Herman
    D. Harry

6. Which of the following combinations appears in Harry's first dream in the novel?

    A. Goethe and a scorpion
    B. Mozart and an automobile
    C. Harry's old colleague and a picture of Goethe
    D. Mozart and Pablo's saxophone

7. What is the name of the public house where Harry first encounters Hermine?

    A. The Steel Helmet
    B. The Magic Flute
    C. The Black Eagle
    D. The Magic Theater

8. According to Goethe, what do immortals like to do?

    A. Make art
    B. Play music
    C. Dance
    D. Joke

9. Why has Harry never danced?

    A. His health has not permitted it
    B. His parents were against it
    C. His religion does not allow it
    D. He is too shy to ask anyone

10. What is the first thing Hermine does when she meets Harry?

    A. Gives him a booklet
    B. Dances with him
    C. Buys him a drink
    D. Wipes his glasses

REVIEW & RESOURCES

11. What does Hermine promise Harry?

    A.   That she will make him happier than he has ever been in his life

    B.   That she will make him something more than the childish joker he has always been

    C.   That she will make him fall in love with her

    D.   That she will make him well respected as an academic again

12. What does Pablo say he will give Harry in exchange for money?

    A.   Opium

    B.   A night with Maria

    C.   His saxophone

    D.   Admission to the Magic Theater

13. Why does Harry not own a gramophone?

    A.   He does not like how they sound

    B.   He dislikes frivolity

    C.   He cannot afford one

    D.   He dislikes music

14. Where does Harry meet Maria?

    A.   His bedroom

    B.   The Fancy Dress Ball

    C.   His first dance

    D.   The Black Eagle

15. Which of the following sexual encounters occurs in the novel?

    A.   Hermine and Maria

    B.   Pablo and Harry

    C.   Pablo, Harry, and Maria

    D.   Harry and Hermine

16. How is Hermine disguised at the masked ball?

    A. As a Spanish dancing girl
    B. As Goethe
    C. As Harry
    D. As Herman

17. What does the clothes ticket tell Harry when he is about to leave the ball?

    A. "Beware Maria"
    B. "Hermine is in hell"
    C. "Do you hear the laughter of the immortals?"
    D. "You are the Steppenwolf"

18. What word does Harry use to describe his dance with Hermine at the end of the ball?

    A. Platonic
    B. Nuptial
    C. Erotic
    D. Dangerous

19. Which of the following doors in the Magic Theater does Harry not enter?

    A. SOLITUDE MADE EASY
    B. ALL GIRLS ARE YOURS
    C. JOLLY HUNTING
    D. HOW ONE KILLS FOR LOVE

20. What does Pablo want Harry to learn to do in the Magic Theater?

    A. Cry
    B. Love
    C. Dance
    D. Laugh

21. What does Harry see in the gigantic mirror to cast off his personality?

    A. All the women he has ever loved in his life
    B. A Steppenwolf
    C. Many Harrys of all ages
    D. Hermine

22. Standing in front of the door in the Magic Theater marked "HOW TO KILL FOR LOVE," what does Harry pull out of his pocket?

    A.   A knife
    B.   The pieces of his life
    C.   His coat ticket
    D.   A mirror

23. Who is Herman?

    A.   Harry's first lover
    B.   Harry's father
    C.   Harry's former colleague
    D.   Harry's boyhood friend

24. Which of the following does Mozart not do the first time Harry meets him?

    A.   Turn a somersault
    B.   Play the violin
    C.   Turn into a comet
    D.   Poke fun at other composers

25. What happens to Hermine after she is stabbed?

    A.   She smiles and tells Harry she loves him
    B.   She shatters into innumerable mirror shards
    C.   Pablo puts her in his pocket
    D.   Mozart turns her into a star

REVIEW & RESOURCES

ANSWER KEY:

1: C; 2: D; 3: B; 4: A; 5: D; 6: A; 7: C; 8: D; 9: B; 10: D; 11: C; 12: B; 13: A; 14: C; 15: A; 16: D; 17: B; 18: B; 19: A; 20: D; 21: C; 22: A; 23: D; 24: B; 25: C

SUGGESTIONS FOR FURTHER READING

CASEBAR, EDWIN F. *Hermann Hesse*. New York: Warner Paperback Library, 1972.

FIELD, G. W. *Hermann Hesse*. New York: Twayne, 1970.

FREEDMAN, RALPH. *Hermann Hesse: Pilgrim of Crisis*. New York: Pantheon Books, 1968.

———. "Person and Persona: The Magic Mirrors of *Steppenwolf*." In *Hesse: A Collection of Critical Essays*. Ed. Theodore Ziolkowski. Englewood Cliffs, New Jersey: Prentice Hall, 1973.

HESSE, HERMANN. *Crisis: Pages from a Diary*. Tr. Ralph Mannheim. New York: Farrar, Straus & Giroux, 1975.

MILECK, JOSEPH. *Herman Hesse: Life, Work, and Criticism*. New York: York Press, 1984.

RICHARDS, DAVID G. *Exploring the Divided Self: Hermann Hesse's* STEPPENWOLF *and Its Critics*. Columbia, South Carolina: Camden House, 1996.

STELZIG, EUGENE L. *Hermann Hesse's Fictions of the Self*. Princeton, New Jersey: Princeton University Press, 1988.

ZIOLKOWSKI, THEODORE. "Hermann Hesse's *Steppenwolf*: A Sonata in Prose." In *Hermann Hesse: A Collection of Criticism*. Ed. Judith Liebman. New York: McGraw-Hill, 1977.

SparkNotes Study Guides:

1984

The Adventures of
  Huckleberry Finn

The Adventures of
  Tom Sawyer

The Aeneid

All Quiet on the
  Western Front

And Then There
  Were None

Angela's Ashes

Animal Farm

Anne of Green Gables

Antony and Cleopatra

As I Lay Dying

As You Like It

The Awakening

The Bean Trees

The Bell Jar

Beloved

Beowulf

Billy Budd

Black Boy

Bless Me, Ultima

The Bluest Eye

Brave New World

The Brothers
  Karamazov

The Call of the Wild

Candide

The Canterbury Tales

Catch-22

The Catcher in the Rye

The Chosen

Cold Mountain

Cold Sassy Tree

The Color Purple

The Count of
  Monte Cristo

Crime and Punishment

The Crucible

Cry, the Beloved
  Country

Cyrano de Bergerac

Death of a Salesman

The Diary of a
  Young Girl

Doctor Faustus

A Doll's House

Don Quixote

Dr. Jekyll and Mr. Hyde

Dracula

Dune

Emma

Ethan Frome

Fahrenheit 451

Fallen Angels

A Farewell to Arms

Flowers for Algernon

The Fountainhead

Frankenstein

The Glass Menagerie

Gone With the Wind

The Good Earth

The Grapes of Wrath

Great Expectations

The Great Gatsby

Gulliver's Travels

Hamlet

The Handmaid's Tale

Hard Times

Harry Potter and the
  Sorcerer's Stone

Heart of Darkness

Henry IV, Part I

Henry V

Hiroshima

The Hobbit

The House of the
  Seven Gables

I Know Why the
  Caged Bird Sings

The Iliad

Inferno

Invisible Man

Jane Eyre

Johnny Tremain

The Joy Luck Club

Julius Caesar

The Jungle

The Killer Angels

King Lear

The Last of the
  Mohicans

Les Misérables

A Lesson Before
  Dying

The Little Prince

Little Women

Lord of the Flies

Macbeth

Madame Bovary

A Man for All Seasons

The Mayor of
  Casterbridge

The Merchant of
  Venice

A Midsummer
  Night's Dream

Moby-Dick

Much Ado About
  Nothing

My Ántonia

Mythology

Native Son

The New Testament

Night

The Odyssey

The Oedipus Trilogy

Of Mice and Men

The Old Man and
  the Sea

The Old Testament

Oliver Twist

The Once and
  Future King

One Flew Over the
  Cuckoo's Nest

One Hundred Years
  of Solitude

Othello

Our Town

The Outsiders

Paradise Lost

The Pearl

The Picture of
  Dorian Gray

A Portrait of the Artist
  as a Young Man

Pride and Prejudice

The Prince

A Raisin in the Sun

The Red Badge of
  Courage

The Republic

Richard III

Robinson Crusoe

Romeo and Juliet

The Scarlet Letter

A Separate Peace

Silas Marner

Sir Gawain and the
  Green Knight

Slaughterhouse-Five

Snow Falling on Cedars

The Sound and the Fury

Steppenwolf

The Stranger

A Streetcar Named
  Desire

The Sun Also Rises

A Tale of Two Cities

The Taming of
  the Shrew

The Tempest

Tess of the
  d'Urbervilles

Their Eyes Were
  Watching God

Things Fall Apart

To Kill a Mockingbird

To the Lighthouse

Treasure Island

Twelfth Night

Ulysses

Uncle Tom's Cabin

Walden

Wuthering Heights

A Yellow Raft in
  Blue Water